THE
BOOK OF...

WHO?

KINGFISHER

KINGFISHER

First published 2010 by Kingfisher
This edition published 2011 by Kingfisher
an imprint of Macmillan Children's Books
a division of Macmillan Publishers Limited
20 New Wharf Road, London N1 9RR
Basingstoke and Oxford
Associated companies throughout the world
www.panmacmillan.com

Illustrated by Del Frost
Concept by Jo Connor

ISBN 978-0-7534-3345-4

Copyright © Macmillan Children's Books 2010

9 8 7 6 5 4 3 2 1
1SPL/0711/LFG/UNTD/140MA

A CIP catalogue for this book is
available from the British Library.

Printed in China

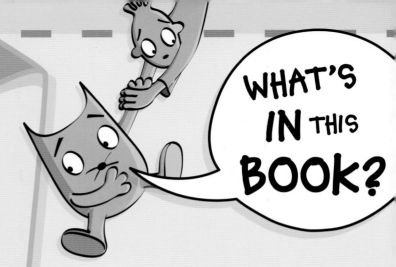

WHAT'S IN THIS BOOK?

WHO OR WHOSE...

6 . . . WERE THE FIRST EXPLORERS?

7 . . . WENT TO SEA IN JUNKS?

8 . . . JOURNEY LASTED 24 YEARS?

9 . . . RAN THE FIRST MARATHON?

10 . . . WERE THE CONQUISTADORS?

11 . . . WERE THE ANCIENT GREEKS?

12 . . . FIRST SAILED AROUND THE WORLD?

13 . . . HAD HIS BEST IDEAS IN THE BATH?

14 . . . CRACKED THE PUZZLE
OF THE LONGEST RIVER?

15 . . . WORKED TO A BEAT?

16 . . . DISCOVERED THE EARTH WAS ROUND?

17 . . . WERE THE FIRST PEOPLE IN SPACE?

18 ... TURNED THE RAIN OFF?

19 ... ENJOYS A MOUTHFUL OF PRICKLES?

20 ... STARTED TALKING?

21 ... SENT THE FIRST RADIO BROADCAST?

22 ... WROTE IN SECRET CODE?

23 ... WRITES WITH A PAINTBRUSH?

24 ... CAN TELL THE TIME WITHOUT A CLOCK?

25 ... TOOK HOURS TO TAKE A PHOTO?

26 ... INVENTED OUR CALENDAR?

27 ... WERE THE ROMANS?

28 ... RULED ROME?

29 ... RULED EGYPT?

30 ... FEET KEEP AN EGG WARM?

31 ... IS THE BEST-DRESSED BIRD?

32 ... IS AT HOME IN A BUBBLE?

33 ... STARTS LIFE WITH A JUMP?

34 ... TONGUE IS LONGER THAN ITS TAIL?

35 ... HORSE HAD EIGHT LEGS?

36 ... HOUSE IS A TRAPDOOR?

37 ... HOUSE IS PAPER THIN?

38 ... WORE STEEPLES ON THEIR HEADS?

39 ... WERE THE MOUNTAIN MEN?

40 ... WAS JOAN OF ARC?

41 ... WAS A TEENAGE WARRIOR?

42 ... RIDES A BUCKING BRONCO?

43 ... TELLS STORIES BY DANCING?

44 ... LIVES IN THE RAINFOREST?

45 ... WERE 'WISE' HUMANS?

46 ... BUILT PALACES IN THE MOUNTAINS?

47 ... ARE THE GREATEST TUNNELLERS?

48 ... FIRST FLUSHED THE TOILET?

49 ... FIRST JUMPED IN THE BATH?

50 ... USED TEA AS MONEY?

51 ... COPIED THE GREEKS?

52 ... WERE THE FIRST FARMERS?

53 ... READS BACK-TO-FRONT?

54 ... SINGING WRECKED SHIPS?

55 ... SINGS UNDER WATER?

56 QUICK-QUIZ QUESTIONS

58 QUICK-QUIZ ANSWERS

60 TRICKY WORDS

62 WHERE TO FIND STUFF

64 FAREWELL

Did you know...

An emperor penguin can hold its breath for 20 minutes when diving for fish.

While we were searching for all those answers, we found out some other pretty interesting things, too. We wrote them all down on these panels – so you can memorize these facts and impress your friends!

We also thought it might be fun to see how much of this shiny new knowledge you can remember – so at the back of the book, on pages 56 and 57, you'll find some Quick-Quiz questions to test you out. It's not as scary as it sounds – we promise it'll be fun. (And besides, we've given you all the answers on pages 58 and 59.)

Are you ready for this big adventure? Then let's go!

QUICK-QUIZ QUESTIONS

WHO WERE THE FIRST EXPLORERS?

Some of the earliest ocean voyages were made by the Polynesian peoples of New Guinea. Nearly 3,500 years ago, they began leaving their homeland to explore the vast Pacific Ocean in nothing bigger than canoes.

Did you know...

Polynesians were not just great explorers, they were also very artistic. Their designs and jewellery are still popular today.

WHO WENT TO SEA IN JUNKS?

Junks are Chinese sailing ships. One of the greatest Chinese explorers was Zheng He. By the early 15th century, his junk ships were the world's biggest and five times the size of European ships.

Did you know...

Zheng He's fleet of junks sailed as far as East Africa and they travelled back with a giraffe!

WHOSE JOURNEY LASTED **24** YEARS?

The Arab explorer Ibn Battuta's adventures began in 1325, when he set out from his home town of Tangier in Morocco. He was so bitten by the travel bug that he didn't return home until 1349!

Did you know...

Ibn Battuta wrote a book about his travels, but his memory was not always that good. He said he had seen hippos with horse-like heads and that the Egyptian pyramids were cone-shaped!

WHO RAN THE FIRST MARATHON?

In 490BCE the ancient Greeks won a battle at Marathon, about 40 kilometres from Athens. A Greek soldier called Pheidippides ran all the way to Athens to tell the citizens the good news. He was so exhausted from running that he collapsed and died.

Did you know...

Marathon races today are 42 kilometres long. It was changed from 40 kilometres at the 1908 Olympic Games, held in London.

WHO WERE THE CONQUISTADORS?

When Columbus discovered the Americas, rumours spread that they were rich in gold. Spanish soldiers began heading there in search of their fortunes. The soldiers were known as Conquistadors, from the Spanish word for 'conqueror', because they were more interested in conquering new lands (and their riches) than exploring them.

Did you know...

The native peoples of the Americas did not use gold as money. Instead, they valued it for its beauty.

WHO WERE the ANCIENT GREEKS?

The Ancient Greeks were people who came from Greece nearly 3,500 years ago. They also lived in lands that we now call Bulgaria and Turkey. Others lived on small, rocky islands in the Aegean Sea, in between Greece and Turkey.

Did you know...

 Greek soldiers fought side by side in tight rows call phalanxes. Each of their shields overlapped the one next to it, making a strong wall of shields that protected them all.

WHO FIRST SAILED AROUND THE WORLD?

A Portuguese explorer named Ferdinand Magellan led the first expedition that sailed around the world, in 1519–1522. He set sail from Spain with five ships and 270 crew members. Magellan was killed during a battle and only one ship returned, carrying 18 men.

Did you know...

When sailing around the Americas, Magellan and his crew ran out of food. They ate rats, leather and sawdust to save themselves from starving.

WHO HAD HIS BEST IDEAS IN THE BATH?

Archimedes was a mathematician who lived in Greece around 250BCE and invented many things, including the catapult. He is famous for shouting 'Eureka!' after having solved a problem he was thinking about while in the bath.

Did you know...

One famous Greek thinker was Digenes. He lived in an old wooden barrel, so people could see he didn't care about money or possessions.

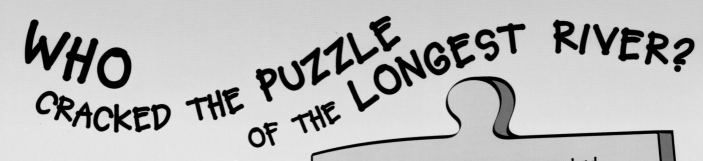

WHO CRACKED THE PUZZLE OF THE LONGEST RIVER?

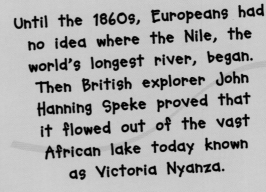

Until the 1860s, Europeans had no idea where the Nile, the world's longest river, began. Then British explorer John Hanning Speke proved that it flowed out of the vast African lake today known as Victoria Nyanza.

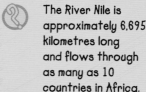

Did you know...

The River Nile is approximately 6,695 kilometres long and flows through as many as 10 countries in Africa.

14

WHO WORKED TO A BEAT?

Rowers on Greek warships worked in time to the music of a drummer or piper. The beat kept the oars moving together and stopped them getting tangled up.

Did you know...

Your heart beats about 90 times every minute. But when you listen to fast-paced music, your heart beat rate speeds up.

WHO WERE THE FIRST PEOPLE IN SPACE?

Did you know...

The first people to walk on the Moon were Americans Neil Armstrong and Edwin 'Buzz' Aldrin, in July 1969.

Russian cosmonaut Yuri Gagarin was the first person ever to travel into space, in April 1961. The first woman to get lift-off was also a Russian – Valentina Tereshkova circled the Earth for nearly three days in June 1963.

WHO TURNED THE RAIN OFF?

A drought can occur when not enough rain falls. This means there is very little drinking water and it is difficult to grow crops. Since the 1970s, the number of serious droughts in the world has doubled.

WHO STARTED TALKING?

Nobody knows how or when people first spoke. They might have started by copying sounds around them, such as the whistling of the wind. By communicating with words, humans could help each other more easily.

Did you know...

There are over 6,900 living languages. The language with the greatest number of speakers is Mandarin Chinese, with over 1 billion speakers!

WHO WROTE IN SECRET CODE?

In medieval times, Scandinavians and Anglo-Saxons sometimes wrote using runes, which were drawn with straight lines. The word rune means 'secret'. Few people could read or write 1,000 years ago. Some thought that anyone who could understand the runes must have magical powers!

Did you know...

The ancient Egyptians used the stalks of papyrus plants to make paper. The word 'paper' comes from 'papyrus'.

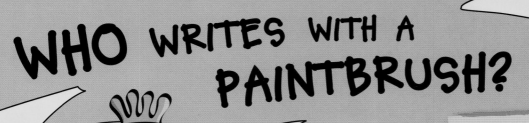

WHO WRITES WITH A PAINTBRUSH?

Did you know...

There are about 50,000 Chinese symbols. School children only have to learn about 5,000 of them, though.

In China and Japan, people sometimes paint words as symbols, slowly and beautifully, with a brush and ink. The art of beautiful handwriting is called calligraphy. Japanese children learn calligraphy at school.

WHO CAN TELL THE TIME WITHOUT A CLOCK?

Inside every one of us there's something called our body clock. It wakes us up every morning, and tells us it's breakfast time. And all through the day we seem to know just when it's time to work, eat and play. As evening comes, we get tired and get ready to sleep.

Did you know...

Some animals sleep through the day and only come out at night. This is called nocturnal behaviour. A badger is a nocturnal animal.

WHO TOOK HOURS TO TAKE A PHOTO?

Cliccccccck!

A Frenchman called Joseph Niépce took the very first photograph in 1826. He had to wait eight hours before the picture was captured on a thin metal plate coated with a sort of tar. The photo showed the view from his window.

Did you know...

The first photograph was of farm buildings and the sky. Niépce called it a heliograph, after the Greek word for Sun – helios.

WHO INVENTED OUR CALENDAR?

More than 2,000 years ago, a Roman ruler called Julius Caesar invented the calendar we use today. He gave each year 365 days, and arranged them in 12 months. Since then, the calendar has hardly changed.

SUN	MON	TUE
1	2	3
8	9	10

Did you know...

The names of our months are taken from the names of Roman gods and rulers. July is named after Julius Caesar.

WHO WERE THE ROMANS?

Did you know...

It would have taken nearly 100 days to ride from one end of the Roman empire to the other. It was a journey of more than 3,000 Roman miles – about 5,000 kilometres.

The Romans were people who came from Rome. About 2,000 years ago they became so powerful that they began to conquer the lands around them. By 100CE they ruled a huge empire, and were one of the mightiest peoples in the ancient world.

WHO RULED ROME?

Over the years, Rome was ruled in three different ways: first by kings, then by a number of officials who were chosen by the people, and finally by an emperor – a ruler of great power and rank.

WHO RULED EGYPT?

The king of Egypt was called the pharaoh. The Egyptians believed that their Sun god Re was the first king of Egypt, and that all the pharaohs after him were his relatives. This made the pharaoh very holy – and very powerful! The people thought he was a god on Earth.

Did you know...

Hatshepsut was a famous female pharaoh. She had to wear badges of royalty, including a false beard made of real hair.

WHOSE FEET KEEP AN EGG WARM?

Every year, in the middle of winter in Antarctica, a female emperor penguin lays one egg, and gives it to her mate to keep warm. He balances the egg between his feet and his feathers, until it is ready to hatch in early spring.

Did you know...

An emperor penguin can hold its breath for 20 minutes when diving for fish.

WHO IS THE BEST-DRESSED BIRD?

Male birds of paradise grow beautiful feathers during the breeding season. When a female comes by, all the males hang upside down to show off their stunning plumage. It is a beauty contest, and the female picks the bird with the finest feathers to be her mate.

Did you know...

The male palm cockatoo attracts a mate by playing a drum beat. It grasps a twig in one foot and beats it against a log.

WHO IS AT HOME IN A BUBBLE?

Baby froghoppers are often called spittlebugs, because they make a bubbly froth very soon after they are born. They hide in this 'cuckoo spit' while they feed and grow.

Did you know...

Spittlebugs can jump up to 100 times their body length!

WHO STARTS LIFE WITH A JUMP?

Mallard ducks often nest in holes in the trees, so their ducklings hatch high above the ground. When their mother calls, they jump out and tumble to the ground. They are so light that they all land safe and sound.

Did you know...

There are more mallard ducks on Earth than any other type of duck.

WHOSE TONGUE IS LONGER THAN ITS TAIL?

The chameleon's sticky-tipped tongue is not just longer than its tail, it is longer than its whole body! The lizard shoots it out incredibly quickly and reels back in a tasty bug.

Did you know...

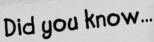

Many lizards can snap off their tails when they're being attacked. A new tail grows back after a few weeks.

WHOSE HORSE HAD EIGHT LEGS?

Did you know...

The Valkyries were warrior women who rode across the sky to carry dead heroes to Odin's heavenly home, Valhalla.

The Vikings called the chief of their gods Odin. They believed he rode an eight-legged horse called Sleipnir, which could gallop across land, sea and sky.

WHOSE HOUSE IS A TRAPDOOR?

The trapdoor spider's burrow has a door with a silk hinge that can open and shut. The spider hides inside, waiting for passing insects. When it hears one, it flings up the trapdoor and grabs its victim.

Did you know...

All spiders can spin silk, but they do not all make webs. The spitting spider catches insects by spitting a sticky gum over them.

Did you know...

There are 1,000 species of paper wasp worldwide, with many living in Australia and North America.

WHOSE HOUSE IS PAPER THIN?

The paper wasp's nest has paper walls. It makes the paper by chewing up strips of wood, which it tears from plants or old fence posts. It spreads the mixture in thin layers to build the nest.

37

WHO WORE STEEPLES ON THEIR HEADS?

All kinds of weird and wonderful headdresses passed in and out of fashion in Europe during the Middle Ages. In the 1400s, women began wearing tall hats called hennins, which looked rather like church steeples. Some hennins were nearly a metre high!

Did you know...

The hats in the Middle Ages were sometimes shaped like a part of an animal. Some were shaped like animals' horns and others like butterflies' wings.

WHO WERE THE MOUNTAIN MEN?

American explorers such as Kit Carson became known as the mountain men during the 1800s. They roamed through the wildest parts of the Rocky Mountains, trapping beavers and other animals for their fur.

WHO WAS JOAN OF ARC?

Joan was a French peasant girl who grew up when England and France were at war. In 1429, at the age of 17, she dressed up as a soldier and helped to free the city of Orleans from an English army. But a year later she was captured and burnt at the stake.

Did you know...

Joan of Arc is the youngest person in history to command a nation's army.

WHO WAS A TEENAGE WARRIOR?

Temujin was the son of a leader of the Mongol people of central Asia. He was born in 1162 and he became a warrior when he was only 13, after his father died. He took the name Genghis Khan. Under his leadership, the Mongols attacked and won many lands in Asia.

Did you know...

In the early 13th century, the Mongol empire covered two per cent of the Earth, and had a population of 100 million.

WHO RIDES A BUCKING BRONCO?

Did you know...

 Another rodeo event is steer roping. A cowhand gallops after a steer (a male bull) and tries to catch it with his lasso.

Cowhands ride in competitions called rodeos. A bronco is an untamed horse, and cowhands test their riding skills by trying to stay on a bronco's back for a few seconds – bareback or with a saddle.

WHO TELLS STORIES BY DANCING?

Did you know...

A three-hour ballet performance needs the same amount of energy as running 29 kilometres.

Ballet is a way of telling a story through music and dance. The sound of the music and the movements of the dancers tell you what's going on as clearly as any story in a book.

43

WHO LIVES IN THE RAINFOREST?

Did you know...

Few tribal children go to school. Their parents teach them how to survive in the rainforest.

Many different tribes live in the world's rainforests. Most build homes and dig out vegetable plots where they grow their own food. The soil in rainforests is poor, though, and the tribes are unable to grow food year after year. After a while, the tribes pack up and move on to another part of the forest.

WHO WERE 'WISE' HUMANS?

Did you know...

The first human-like creatures lived about 4.5 million years ago. They were called Australopithecus.

Modern humans are clever, which is why our scientific name is Homo sapiens, meaning 'wise human'. The first Homo sapiens evolved in Africa almost 200,000 years ago.

WHO BUILT PALACES IN THE MOUNTAINS?

Did you know...

The site Machu Picchu had been deserted for over 400 years, until the American explorer Hiram Bingham rediscovered it in 1911.

Back in the 1400s, the Incas ruled over vast parts of the South Andes Mountains in America. They built amazing stone towns and palaces in the mountains, including the mysterious Machu Picchu.

WHO ARE THE GREATEST TUNNELLERS?

At the moment, the greatest tunnel builders are the Japanese. Their 53.8km-long Seikan railway tunnel links the Honshu and Hokkaido islands. In 2017, the Swiss Gotthard Base Tunnel under the Alps will be open. It will be an amazing 57.1km long.

Did you know...

From planning to opening, the Seikan railway tunnel took 42 years to construct.

Did you know...

Nearly 100 years ago, toilets that flushed were highly prized pieces of furniture. They were decorated with fruit, flowers and shells.

WHO FIRST FLUSHED THE TOILET?

Almost 400 years ago, Sir John Harrington built a flushing toilet for his godmother, Queen Elizabeth I of England. In those days very few homes had water pipes or drains, so ordinary people had to carry on using chamber pots.

WHO FIRST JUMPED IN THE BATH?

Did you know...

Almost 500 years ago, the Chinese used pigs' hair to make the first toothbrushes!

In ancient times, the people of Greece, Rome and the Indus Valley in Pakistan enjoyed a bath. But, as time went by, baths went out of fashion and many people never even washed. They used perfumes to cover up the smell!

WHO USED TEA AS MONEY?

Did you know...

The Chinese first used paper money about 1,200 years ago. They printed some of the notes on the bark of mulberry trees.

People in Tibet and China once used tea pressed into blocks as money. Before coins were invented, people used to swap things like shells, beads or grain for the goods they wanted.

WHO COPIED THE GREEKS?

About 2,000 years ago, the Romans marched into Greece. They conquered its armies and added its lands to their own empire. But Roman people respected the Greek ways of life. They admired Greek poetry, plays, buildings and art. They copied many Greek ideas and used them to improve their own ways of life.

Did you know...

There were more than 40 religious holidays in Athens each year. There are paintings of these festivals on Greek potteries and wine jars.

WHO WERE THE FIRST FARMERS?

Did you know...

The first crops were wheat and barley, and the first farm animals were goats and sheep.

Farming began about 10,000 years ago, when people in the Middle East began saving the seeds of wild plants to sow as their own crops. Growing their own food meant that farmers could stay in the same place all year round.

WHO READS BACK-TO-FRONT?

To read a book in Arabic or Hebrew you have to work from right to left. So if this book were in Arabic, the first page would be where the index is now.

Did you know...

The oldest printed book in the world is believed to be 'The Diamond Sutra', which dates from 868CE.

WHOSE SINGING WRECKED SHIPS?

In fairy tales, mermaids were magical creatures – half-woman and half-fish – who lived in the sea near dangerous, rocky coasts. They sang so sweetly that the sailors who heard them forgot everything else – including how to steer their ship away from rocks!

Did you know...

The patron saint of music is Saint Cecilia. In pictures of her, she usually has a miniature organ on her lap.

WHO SINGS UNDER WATER?

Did you know...

Humpback whale calves do not stop growing until they are ten years old.

Humpback whales seem to sing to each other under the ocean. It is thought they are singing to attract a mate. No other animal's song lasts as long as the humpback's, which can be heard hundreds of kilometres away.

QUICK-QUIZ QUESTIONS

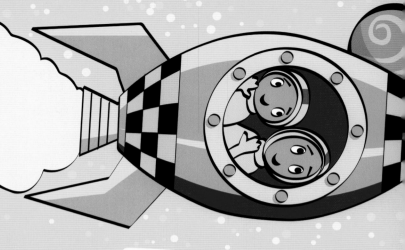

1. Which ocean did Polynesian people explore nearly 3,500 years ago?

2. How many kilometres is a modern marathon?

3. Which language does the word 'Conquistador' come from?

4. Where did the Greek thinker Digenes live?

5. Where does the River Nile begin?

6. Name the two types of eclipse that can occur.

7. What is a drought?

8. Which language has the greatest number of speakers?

9. Unscramble ALL CHIP GRAY to spell the art of beautiful writing.

10. What does the Greek word 'helios' mean?

11. The month July is named after which Roman ruler?

12. Hatshepsut was a famous male pharaoh. True or false?

13. Where do emperor penguins live?

14. What is another name for a froghopper?

15. Unscramble OCEAN HELM to spell the name of a sticky-tongued lizard?

16. All spiders can spin silk. True or false?

17. What is the name for a tall hat worn by women in the 1400s?

18. How old was Temujin when he became a warrior?

19. What competitions do cowhands take part in?

20. What is the scientific name for modern humans?

21. Which mountain range is home to the Inca site Machu Picchu?

22. What did the Chinese use to make the first toothbrushes?

23. What items were used by people in Tibet and China to buy goods?

24. Which languages read from right to left?

25. Which whale's song can travel many kilometres?

QUICK-QUIZ ANSWERS

1. The Pacific Ocean.

2. A modern marathon is 42 kilometres.

3. Spanish.

4. In a barrel.

5. It flows out of lake Victoria Nyanza, in Africa.

6. Lunar and solar eclipses.

7. A drought is a severe shortage of rainfall.

8. Mandarin Chinese, with more than 1 billion speakers.

9. ALL CHIP GRAY = calligraphy.

10. Sun.

11. Julius Caesar.

12. False. Hatshepsut was female.

13. Antarctica.

14. A spittle bug.

15. OCEAN HELM = chameleon.

16. True.

17. A hennin.

18. He was 13 years old.

19. Rodeos.

20. Homo sapiens.

21. The Andes in South America.

22. Pigs' hair.

23. Tea, shells, beads and grain.

24. Arabic and Hebrew.

25. The humpback whale's.

TRICKY WORDS

ANGLO-SAXONS
People who lived in England from the 5th century CE to 1066.

ANTARCTICA
Earth's icy, southernmost area around the South Pole.

BREEDING SEASON
The time when male and female animals come together to produce offspring.

BROADCAST
To send out a programme over radio waves so it can be heard on a radio or watched on a television. A programme sent this way is also called a broadcast.

CATAPULT
A weapon that is used to throw something, such as a rock, through the air quickly.

CITIZENS
The people who live in a particular area, such as a town, city or country.

COMMUNICATING
Sharing information with someone, such as by speaking or writing.

CONQUER
To win and take control of something.

COSMONAUT
The Russian word for an astronaut. An astronaut is a person who travels into space to find out more about it.

CROPS
Plants such as wheat, corn or potatoes that are grown over large areas in fields for food.

DROUGHT
A long period of time in which no rain falls. Rivers can dry up and plants can die without water. Food and drinking water may be hard to find in areas suffering from drought.

EMPIRE
A large area of land, usually several countries, ruled by one government. The Romans had a huge empire.

EXPEDITION
An organized journey, such as one that travels to explore part of a country.

FLEET
A group of ships sailing together.

INCA
People who lived from 700 to 450 years ago in South America. The centre of their empire was in Peru.

INVENTOR
A person who is the first to think of or create something.

LASSO
A long rope with a loop at one end. It is thrown so that the loop falls around an animal's neck.

LUNAR
Describing something that involves the Moon.

MAJOR
Something that is important or serious.

MIDDLE AGES
The time period in Europe between 476 and 1500CE. These years are also called 'medieval times'.

NATIVE PEOPLE
The first people who originally lived in a country, before settlers arrived from other countries.

NOCTURNAL
Describing something that happens at night. Nocturnal animals are active at night.

OLYMPIC GAMES
First begun in ancient Greece, the Olympic Games are sporting events that take place every four years. Athletes from all over the world take part to win gold, silver or bronze medals.

POSSESSIONS
Objects that are owned.

PYRAMID
Large, stone buildings with four triangular sides. Pyramids were built as tombs for ancient Egyptian kings and queens, who were buried with all their riches.

RANK
A person's position in a group, such as in an army.

ROMANS
Ancient people from Italy who lived around 2,000 years ago in Europe, Africa and Asia.

SCANDINAVIA
A region in northern Europe that includes Denmark, Norway and Sweden.

SILK
Fine threads that are made by insects and woven together to make a soft, smooth and strong material.

SOLAR
Describing something that involves the Sun.

SYMBOL
A shape or design that is drawn to show an idea of something, such as a word.

TAR
A black, sticky substance from rocks. Tar is used to coat the surface of roads.

VIKING
People from Scandinavia who sailed and battled with people across the world, especially in north-eastern Europe, from the 8th to 11th centuries.

WHERE TO FIND STUFF

A

Africa 7, 14, 45
Aldrin, Edwin 'Buzz' 17
Anglo-Saxons 22
animals 24, 38, 39, 52, 55
Antarctica 30
Armstrong, Neil 17
Asia 41
Australia 18, 37

B

ballet 43
baths 49
battles 9, 12
birds 30, 31, 33
body clocks 24
books 8, 53

C

cacti 19
Caesar, Julius 26
calendars 26
calligraphy 23
catapults 13
chameleons 34
children 23, 44
China 7, 23, 49, 50
Conquistadors 10
crops 18, 52

D

droughts 18
ducks 33

E

Earth 16
eclipses 16
eggs 30
Egyptians, ancient 22, 29
explorers 6, 7, 8, 12, 14, 39, 46

F

farming 52
feathers 30, 31
food 12, 44, 52
froghoppers 32

G

Gagarin, Yuri 17
Galapagos Islands 19
giraffes 7
gods 26, 29
gold 10
Greeks, ancient 9, 11, 13, 15, 16, 49, 51

HIJ

hats 38
He, Zheng 7
heart beats 15
heliographs 25
hippos 8
homo sapiens 45
horses 35, 42
Incas 46
insects 19, 32, 34, 36
inventors 21